D0330731

AROUND
THE TABLE

AROUND THE TABLE

Family Stories of
SHOLOM ALEICHEM

Selected and Translated by
ALIZA SHEVRIN

Illustrated by Toby Gowing

CHARLES SCRIBNER'S SONS · NEW YORK
Maxwell Macmillan Canada · Toronto
Maxwell Macmillan International
New York · Oxford · Singapore · Sydney

SOMERSET COUNTY LIBRARY
BRIDGEWATER, N. J. 08807

Translation copyright © 1991 by Aliza Shevrin
Original Yiddish version copyright © 1918, 1919 Olga Rabinowitz
Illustrations copyright © 1991 by Toby Gowing

All rights reserved. No part of this book may be reproduced or transmitted in any
form or by any means, electronic or mechanical, including photocopying,
recording, or by any information storage and retrieval system, without permission in
writing from the Publisher.

Charles Scribner's Sons Books for Young Readers
Macmillan Publishing Company
866 Third Avenue, New York, NY 10022

Maxwell Macmillan Canada, Inc.
1200 Eglinton Avenue East, Suite 200
Don Mills, Ontario M3C 3N1

Macmillan Publishing Company is part of
the Maxwell Communication Group of Companies.

First Edition   10 9 8 7 6 5 4 3 2 1
Printed in the United States of America

Library of Congress Cataloging-in-Publication Data
Sholem Aleichem, 1859–1916.
[Short stories. English. Selections]
Around the table : family stories of Sholom Aleichem / selected and translated
by Aliza Shevrin ; illustrated by Toby Gowing. — 1st ed.   p.   cm.
Summary: Presents retellings of five Sholom Aleichem stories which depict
families observing the rituals and traditions of Jewish holidays together.
ISBN 0-684-19237-3
1. Children's stories, Yiddish—Translations into English.
2. Children's stories, English—Translations from Yiddish.
[1. Fasts and feasts—Judaism—Fiction.   2. Family life—Fiction.
3. Jews—Fiction.   4. Short stories.]   I. Shevrin, Aliza.
II. Gowing, Toby, ill.   III. Title.
PZ7.R110Ar   1991   [Fic]—dc20   90-49273

For My Grandchildren

ILENE
JULIE
ARIEL
ERIC
SUZANNAH
—A.S.

Contents

AROUND
THE TABLE

Introduction

I am happy to present this second collection of Sholom Aleichem's stories for children. It is always a pleasure to read through his stories in order to select the best ones to translate, and I always have a difficult time because I want all of them available to young readers. I call these "stories for children," but you must realize that Sholom Aleichem wrote for children of all ages, as did other writers of "children's" stories, like Lewis Carroll. These stories and tales can be read and enjoyed by everyone. They are best enjoyed when read aloud, and if something needs explaining, all the better. That provides a good excuse for an adult who might feel odd reading the stories to himself or herself.

Sholom Aleichem is the pen name for Solomon

Rabinowitz, the great and beloved Yiddish writer. It is the customary Hebrew greeting and means literally, "Peace unto you." He was born in Russia in 1859 and died in New York in 1916. He wrote many, many stories, plays, and novels in the Jewish language, Yiddish. In Europe, his readers were able to read them in Yiddish, a wonderfully expressive language, highly idiomatic and sprinkled with folk sayings. Now, unfortunately, few people speak Yiddish fluently, and so it is necessary for people like myself, who grew up speaking Yiddish and are also fluent in English, to translate Sholom Aleichem into English so that many more people can read and enjoy his writings.

How does a translator translate? Each language has its own way of saying things, its own rhythm and sound, its own distinctive vocabulary that gives the language its own character. Think of English or whatever other language you may speak. If you know another language, try to rewrite something—exactly, as if the author were writing it—in that other language. You will want to have all the words mean the same, but sometimes one language does not have the same vocabulary or way of forming a sentence as the other. Sometimes, even if it is correct, it doesn't seem to *sound* right. Then it becomes the task of the translator to find equivalents, words that come as close to the original meaning as possible and that have the same "flavor."

There are times when something is almost untranslatable, even a familiar Yiddish word like *mentsh*. In the story "The Purim Dinner," the mother tells the young boy to "sit up like a person" when he goes to his rich uncle's house for the Purim dinner. In Yiddish, the words are, *Zitz vi a mentsh,* which means he should behave like a human being, properly and with pride. This word is so Yiddish that the word *person* doesn't quite mean the same thing, although technically that is correct. But no mother in the world would tell her rambunctious son to "sit like a human being, properly and with pride." It doesn't *sound* right. And so the translator reads and rereads the work until she literally "tastes" it, and then she does her best, word by word, over and over, hoping to have done as much justice to the author's work as possible. Oddly enough, the best compliment for a translator is the reader's unawareness that a story has been translated.

All the stories in this collection are about families, as are most of Sholom Aleichem's stories. And when does a family get together mostly if not for meals, around the table? And what better opportunity for a good story—happy, funny, or sad—than at holiday time, when families prepare food, visit one another, sit down together to eat, and sometimes have quarrels? Rich or poor, small or large, the family observes the rituals and traditions of the Jewish holidays together.

Usually it is the children who are at the center of

Sholom Aleichem's stories. He himself was the head of a large family, and surely many of the stories were written especially for his children and grandchildren to enjoy. Perhaps the stories also taught them some of the traditions that Jewish families follow in celebrating the holidays, each of which commemorates an important event in Jewish history. They also conveyed the basic Jewish values of family loyalty and interdependency. I hope this collection will serve the same purpose, although by now some of the customs have changed. Children rarely go from relative to relative collecting Chanukah money. Families are far-flung, and children expect, and usually receive, a Chanukah present for each of the eight nights of Chanukah. Moreover, children are not expected to be silent, perfectly behaved guests at a holiday dinner. Nevertheless, the feeling of togetherness in sharing a celebration around the table is basic to the Jewish family, as is the spirit of generosity even when there may not be enough food to go around.

In the only story not narrated by a child, "The Happiness Children Bring," the poor father derives enormous pleasure (another untranslatable word for pleasure is *nakhas*, which also means gratification or joy) from his large, poor family even though he must make great sacrifices to help them in times of difficulty. But as he says, "When it comes to the happiness children bring, I have more than the richest rich man in Kasrilevka!"

Why do all these stories contain elements of sadness and things ending badly, one wonders? We always think of Sholom Aleichem as a great humorist in the style of Mark Twain. The word *bittersweet* is frequently used in describing his writing, but it seems sometimes to be more bitter than sweet. Perhaps Sholom Aleichem himself experienced the bitterness of growing up in poverty in Russia. Life was indeed difficult in the 1880s for Jewish families, and there was little time or energy for understanding a child's emotional needs and problems. Beyond the absolutes of education, the basic minimal physical necessities, and adhering to religious requirements, children were left to manage and to entertain themselves as well as they could while the family struggled to survive poverty and persecution.

Sholom Aleichem grew up in a large, poor family in a small village in Russia. His own mother was self-sacrificing, compassionate, and loving, while the stepmother who took his mother's place after her death when he was twelve was frequently selfish and uncaring. Both mother and stepmother were models for many of his female characters. One has the feeling that without his sense of humor, without his ability to laugh at what was happening, life would have been unbearable for him. And according to his descendants, he grew up to be a loving and kind father and grandfather.

There is one important thing that needs some explaining and may be confusing to readers: In two of the stories, when the father is making the blessing before dinner, he communicates or answers questions by making nonsense sounds, such as "Ee-aw-aw!" and "Ee-o-eh!" That is because once he starts the blessing, he cannot speak until the prayer is completed, and if necessary, he must use sounds to convey what he means.

I am lucky to have a large family of four children and five grandchildren, so far. We also enjoy many happy times around the table, especially at holidays. I wish to dedicate this book to them. I also am grateful to my husband, Howie, who shares my devotion to our family as well as the *nakhas* and fun. He helped me with these stories, as he does with all my work, and I thank him with all my heart.

Aliza Shevrin
Ann Arbor, Michigan

ONE

The Happiness Children Bring

Let me tell you right off that I am not a rich man. Far, far from a rich man. I have next to nothing. True, I have a family, we have our own place, if you can call it that. You can imagine what sort of place it is—worthless! But when it comes to the happiness children bring, I can truly boast of having, blessed be His name, more than the richest rich man in Kasrilevka! And when there is a holiday, I tell you, and all the children gather together, sons and daughters, sons- and daughters-in-law, and all the grandchildren—well, who can be compared to me?

For instance, take the Purim feast.

How would it feel, I ask you, for just you and your wife to sit down at the Purim table?

Imagine it for a second. We've already finished the fish served in broth, the noodles, the *tzimmes*, and so on and so on—but what does it all amount to? Absolutely nothing, that's what, absolutely nothing! A horse, forgive the comparison, must eat too. But a human being is not a horse. And especially a Jew. And especially when it's a holiday. And especially when it's a holiday like Purim!

First let's consider the children.

Eight, that's how many I have, long life to them, every one of them married. (There used to be twelve, but four of them are gone, may those remaining live to a ripe old age). Half of them are sons, half are daughters; four sons-in-law and four daughters-in-law. So it adds up to no fewer than sixteen.

Then consider all the grandchildren, long life to them!

No complaints. All the daughters and all the daughters-in-law, thank God, have babies every year; one has eleven, another nine, another seven. There isn't one among them who is barren, God forbid.

But with one son, the middle one, I did have some trouble: For a while my daughter-in-law didn't have any children—none at all. She didn't, and she didn't, and that was that! And it became a long, drawn-out story involving doctors, the rabbi, even a Gypsy fortune-teller. Nothing helped.

Not to waste words, it was decided: a divorce.

Well, divorce is serious business. But when it came

down to actually getting the divorce, what do you think happens? My daughter-in-law won't have it!

Why won't she have it? She loves him, she says.

"Idiot! Why do you listen to her when she says she loves you?" I say to my son, the middle one. He says, "I love her too." What do you say to that genius? I say, "Children." He says, "Love!" What do you make of such a simpleton?

Not to waste words, they *didn't* divorce. And God helped out. It's been six years since she started having babies. Year in, year out, she showers me with another grandchild!

If you could only see my grandchildren—every one of them bright, one prettier than the next, their faces shining! I tell you, treasures!

And what scholars they are! Is it a passage from the Bible you want recited? You'll get it by heart. And how they read and write Yiddish and Russian and German and French!

When I need to have a letter read or an address written, or whatever, a battle royal breaks out among them: "*Zayde'nyu*, let me do it! *Zayde'nyu*, I'll do it!"

What's that? You want to know how we manage? Ah, we have a mighty God! He always has His way. Sometimes this way, sometimes that way. Sometimes for the better, sometimes for the worse. Usually for the worse. You struggle and somehow you make it through the year, as long as you stay healthy. Don't you agree?

Things were not going too badly for my eldest son. He was living in a village, it was in Zlodyevka, and he was making a decent living. But when the residency law changed, they requested that he politely leave. He did whatever he could to prove the new law did not apply to him. He brought proof showing he had been living there from practically the beginning of time. Not to waste words, he didn't have a prayer of a chance. They drove him out, and to this day he can't get over it. He lives with me, together with his wife and children. What choice do I have?

And as for my other son, nothing seems to go right for the poor fellow. Whatever he does, he runs into bad luck. As they say, "Let him drop his bread, it'll be with the buttered side down." Let him buy grain, the market will be flooded with grain. Let him deal in oxen, they'll die off. Let him sell firewood, and it'll be a warm winter. No luck! If he were to look into the river, all the fish would go belly-up. I thought it over and said to him, "Why don't you just pack up your wife and children and move in with me? Don't ask any questions. Just do it!"

My third son was getting by but lost everything in the Great Fire, may it never happen to anyone. He came out of it naked as the day he was born and still had big troubles with the authorities over his military service—and lawsuits! It was bad! Now he and his whole gang live with me. What else can I do?

But my youngest son is doing quite well, thank

God. What does "quite well" mean? He himself doesn't have money, but he has a rich father-in-law. Well, he's not that rich. He has many businesses; he's something of a finagler. He has his fingers in many pies. He's a big wheeler-dealer, may the One above protect us from his kind! He wheels and deals so long until he wheels and deals himself and everyone else around him into a pickle. And then what happens? Somehow he knows how to wheel and deal his way out every time, the rascal. How many times did he lose all his money as well as the children's money? So I say to him, "Why do you have to use my son's money?" He says, "What business is it of yours? Did you put in a lot of your own cash?" I say, "But my son is still my child." He says, "And my daughter isn't my child?" I say, "Ha!" He says, "Beh!" I say, "Never mind!" He says, "That's that!" Tit for tat. I call my son off to the side and say to him, "Spit on your rich father-in-law, the wheeler-dealer, and move in with me. We'll manage with whatever God grants us, so long as we're together."

Listen, when it comes to sons-in-law, I have no luck at all. But really absolutely none at all! Oh, I don't have anything against them, and I'm not ashamed of them, God forbid. I have, you may believe me, the kind of sons-in-law that the wealthiest man doesn't possess. Fine lads, from good families, respectable young men with good heads on their shoulders.

One of them is a bit too refined and overindulged, comes from a distinguished family, but he's gifted, a fine scholar who sits day in, day out and studies. I've been supporting him since the wedding. If you were to see him, you yourself would say it would be a sin to let him out on his own—what would become of him?

The other son-in-law doesn't come from as distinguished a family, but he is one in a million. Let me describe him for you. What would you like to know about him? He can write, read, do arithmetic, sing, dance, you name it. And when it comes to chess, say the word, can he play! Still and all, if it's not in the cards . . . How did King Solomon put it? "The clever ones go barefoot." I did everything I could to help him make a living. He tried his hand at running an estate; he was a shopkeeper, a teacher, and a matchmaker. Nothing worked, no matter what he tried! He lives in my house now with his children. I won't throw my own daughter out on the street!

I have one more son-in-law, not quite as clever, but certainly no ignoramus. He has a good head on his shoulders, writes a fine hand, can read a page of Commentaries, and has a way with words. When he speaks, each word is a gem, a pleasure to listen to!

He has one weakness. He is too delicate, almost wraithlike. I mean, he's not overly healthy. If you were to look at him, you wouldn't see anything wrong. You wouldn't know what the problem is. It's that he sweats. And on top of that, he coughs! It's been some time now since he caught a terrible cough with a kind of wheeze to it, and it's hard for him to catch his breath. The doctors tell him to drink milk and go to Boiberik. That's where all the sick people go, they say. There one finds a certain grove of trees that cures coughs. So I figure next summer, if God gives us life, we'll drive up to Boiberik with him. In the meantime, till he gets well, he and his children are, naturally, on my shoulders. What else can I do?

And then I have a son-in-law who is just your ordinary fellow, a hard-working young man, but not a plain working man, nor a tailor, nor a shoemaker, nor a student.

He deals in fish. His father deals in fish. His grandfather dealt in fish. His whole family knows nothing but fish and fish and more fish!

What I mean to say is that they are altogether honest Jews, respectable, but common people.

You will ask: How does a son-in-law like that come to me? There must be a story connected with it. As they say, "In a river there are all sorts of pike." It was probably my daughter's fate that she deserved *that* kind of man.

Oh, I have nothing against him; my daughter is very happy with him because he is by nature a good person, a rare jewel, absolutely devoted to us, I tell you. Whatever he earns he gives her, and he helps my other sons-in-law and sons as much as he possibly can. What is there to say? He toils almost entirely for us and holds us in high esteem because he knows very well, you understand, who *he* is and who *we* are; he is he and we are, after all, we! You can't just shrug that off.

When it occasionally happens that we get together and my children start discussing one of the finer points of a Torah portion, a judgment in the Shulkhan Arukh, the laws governing the life of an Orthodox Jew, or a difficult passage of the Commentaries, the poor boy has to sit in silence, because for him it's all a mystery.

Of course he can take pride in having such in-laws and should work hard for them! Isn't that so? Isn't it right and fitting?

Now that you are a bit acquainted with my family, you can better understand what joy there is in my house when a festive holiday like Purim comes, and all the children and all the grandchildren sit down around the table, and we chant the prayer over the beautiful, large, glistening Purim egg bread made with saffron and studded with raisins and eat the delicious, peppery sweet fish with horseradish, the tasty, long, golden noodles and the rich broth, and we have a little drink, if God grants a flask of a really good cherry brandy or a glass of fine plum brandy, so long as we can get it, and in a pinch we can always have an ordinary shnapps, no complaints. And we start to sing. I start off with the traditional *Shoshanas Yaakov*, and they repeat, *Shoshanas Yaakov!*

And once more, *Shoshanas Yaakov!*

And the children chime in: *Tzehala v'sameykha!*

And the little scamps, the grandchildren, with their high-pitched voices, pipe in: *Or l'yihudim! Or l'yihudim! Or l'yihudim!*

And then someone starts dancing. At a time like that, who can be compared to me? Who cares about the millionaire Brodsky? Never mind Rothschild. I am a king. As I am a Jew, I am a king!

A rich man, I tell you, I am not. But with the happiness children bring, blessed be His name, I have more than the richest rich man in Kasrilevka!

• TWO •

The Purim Dinner

"I don't know what's going to become of this child! He's such a weakling, such a nothing, a crybaby, God help me! A child who just won't stop crying!"

That's what my mother was muttering to herself as she was dressing me in my holiday outfit, all the while poking me in the ribs or jabbing me in the back or tugging my ear or yanking my hair or pinching me hard, and she expected me to laugh, not cry. She buttoned me from top to bottom into my little black Sabbath coat, which had long been too tight for me, so that my eyes almost popped out of my head; and the sleeves were far too short, and my chapped hands looked much too large for them, as though they were swollen, something my mother could not stand.

"Look at those paws!" She slapped me across the

hands so I would draw them closer to me and not have them so visible. "When you sit at Uncle Hertz's table I want you to keep your hands hidden out of sight. Do you hear what I'm telling you? And I don't want you blushing like Yadvucha, the peasant girl, and I don't want you staring wide-eyed like a tomcat. Do you hear what I'm saying to you? And I want you to sit up like a person—but it's that nose, oy, that no-ose! Give me that no-ose of yours, let me put it right!"

So long as my nose was called a nose I could put up with it, but since it became for my mother a "no-ose" and she took to "putting it right," life became unbearable for it, my poor nose. I don't know what sin my nose, more than any other part of my body, had committed to turn my mother into its bitter enemy. It seems to me it was a nose like all other noses—a bit fleshy, a bit reddish, a bit tilted up, and sometimes it liked to be a bit damp. So what of it? Did she need to make life so miserable for it? You can believe me, there were times when I begged God to rid me of it. I prayed it would fall off—the devil with it, and let there be an end to it! I used to imagine that one fine morning I would wake up without a nose and would go over to my mother after breakfast. She would take hold of me. "God in heaven! Where is your nose?" I would feel all over my face and look at my mother as if she were out of her mind and feel secretly triumphant. Serves her right! Let her

see what her son looked like without a nose!

Childish ideas! Foolish fantasies! God didn't hear my pleas. The nose grew, my mother was always "putting it right," and both the nose and I were miserable. But my poor nose suffered most of all at holiday time, like on Purim, when we were preparing to go to Uncle Hertz's for the Purim dinner.

Uncle Hertz was not only the wealthiest member of our family, he was the most prominent citizen in our village. Here and in all the surrounding villages his name was everywhere to be heard. You will not be surprised to learn that he owned a pair of lively horses and rode in his own impressive carriage, the wheels making such a racket that everyone in the village would run out to see Uncle Hertz riding by. And Uncle Hertz sat right up front with his fine brass-colored beard and fierce gray eyes, swaying back and forth, peering down at everyone through his silver spectacles, as if to say, How do you vermin compare yourselves to me? I am Hertz, the rich man, and I ride in my carriage while you poor Kasrilikes, paupers, beggars, crawl in the mud!

I don't know about anybody else, but I personally detested Uncle Hertz so much that I could hardly bear looking at that red face of his with those fat cheeks, its brass-colored beard, and silver spectacles, his fat paunch with the massive golden chain draped across it, and the round silk yarmulke on his head. And above all, I hated that little cough of his! He had his own special little cough, which was accompanied by a shrug of the shoulders, a toss of the head upward, and a pursing of his lips, as if to say, Show respect! I, Hertz, am coughing, not because, God forbid, I have caught cold, but just because I feel like coughing. So I cough. . . .

I don't understand our family. Why did they get all worked up when Purim came and we all had to go to Uncle Hertz's for the dinner? It seems they loved him as much as they loved a bad headache, and even my mother, who was his own sister, was herself not overly fond of him, because when the older children weren't at home (apparently she didn't care what she said in front of me), she blessed Uncle Hertz with the strangest blessings. She wished that by next year he would find himself in her circumstances. But let someone else say a bad word about Uncle Hertz, and she would scratch his eyes out. I once heard how my father happened inadvertently to refer to Uncle Hertz in a slightly derogatory manner. Do you think he was blackening my uncle's name? He merely remarked to my mother, "What's new? Has your brother Hertz come back yet, or not?" Well, she really laced into my poor father so that he didn't know what had hit him.

"What is this *my* Hertz? What kind of talk is that? What kind of expression is that? What is this *my*, eh?"

"Yours. Whose else is he, mine?" My father feebly

tried to defend himself, but it did no good because my mother was on the attack:

"So if he's mine, so what of it? So, mine! You don't benefit from it? He's not good enough for your family? You had to share your inheritance with him, is that it? You never received any favors from him, is that it?"

"Who said I didn't?" My father attempted to placate her, but it didn't work; my mother would not stop her onslaught.

"Maybe you have better brothers than I have, is that it? Handsomer, more respectable, richer, is that it?"

"Calm down! Enough!" my father cried, clapping on his hat and fleeing the house. He had lost the battle and my mother had been victorious, as always. She was always victorious. She always won out, not because she was right, but because Uncle Hertz was rich and we were his poor relations.

What was Uncle Hertz to us really? Did he support us? Or did he do us big favors? This I cannot tell you because I don't know. I only know that everyone in the house, from the oldest to the youngest, was scared to death of Uncle Hertz. Already two weeks before Purim we were beginning to prepare for Uncle Hertz's dinner. My older brother, Moshe-Abraham, a young man with pale, sunken cheeks and dark eyes absorbed in thought, would stroke his sidelocks whenever Uncle Hertz's dinner was mentioned.

And you can imagine what was going on with my two sisters, Miriam-Reyzl and Chana-Rochl, one of whom was already engaged to be married. They had begun having dresses sewn according to the latest fashion for the dinner at Uncle Hertz's and had bought pretty combs and ribbons for their hair. They had desperately wanted to have their shoes mended, but my mother had to put it off till after Pesach, though it grieved her very much that they had to go practically barefoot. She had her hands full with my sister Miriam-Reyzl, who was especially upset for fear that her young man might notice she was wearing torn shoes. She was having enough trouble as it was with her fiancé. Not enough that he was a low sort who fancied himself a bookkeeper when he was just a clerk in a shop, but he put on airs and had high pretensions, insisting that my sister get all decked out in the latest style like a princess.

Every Shabbos afternoon this clerk would appear at the house, sit himself down with both my sisters at the window, and they would chat, mostly about fine clothes, new outfits, shiny boots and shoes, strange hats with feathers, and parasols with frills, as well as embroidered pillowcases with red lace inserts, and a white sheet over a well-made, authentic feather bed that kept you really warm when you slept at night during the winter. And I could see my sister Miriam-Reyzl suddenly turning as red as a beet. Miriam-Reyzl had this knack: Whenever she felt embarrassed over the least little thing, her face would flush bright red. And should he happen to glance at her feet, she would quickly hide them under the chair, apparently afraid he might notice her worn-down heels and threadbare tops.

"Are you ready to go to the dinner?" my mother asked my father the day after the reading of the Megillah.

"What's there to getting ready?" he answered her, and put on his long Sabbath jacket. "Where are the children?"

"The children are almost ready," my mother replied, though she knew all too well that the children, that is, my sisters, were far from ready. They were still washing their hair, rubbing it with almond oil to make it shine, combing one another, beautifying themselves, putting on their new dresses, and polishing their shoes with fat so as to make them shine, too. But what good were shiny shoes when the heels, the poor heels, were entirely run-down and the toes were almost showing? What would my sisters do if, God forbid, the bridegroom were to notice it? And out of spite, an ill wind blew in the clerk himself, wearing a new suit, a stiffly starched collar, and a modish green cravat. Out of his stiffly starched cuffs poked two meaty, red hands with ink-stained fingernails. His recently shorn hair stuck out every which way. From his bosom pocket he drew a white, stiffly starched handkerchief reeking of spices and cloves that tickled my nose, and I began sneezing, causing two buttons to go flying off my jacket. My mother hit the ceiling.

"Did you ever in your life see a child who can't keep a button on his clothes! May *you* not fall apart, God forbid!" she cried, grabbing a needle and thread and quickly sewing the sprung-off buttons back on. And when all of us were ready, we set forth for Uncle Hertz's Purim dinner.

At the head of the procession, hoisting up the skirts of his long coat, went my father; after him, my mother, in a pair of men's boots because the mud was very deep; after her, both my sisters with parasols in hand (maybe you can tell me why you need a parasol at Purim time?); after them, my older brother, Moshe-Abraham, who strode over the mud holding my hand, seeking a dry spot, a path, but kept stepping right into the deepest, muddiest part, jumping back as if singed—ooh-ah! Alongside us slogged our bridegroom, the clerk, in a pair of new high galoshes, the only one wearing galoshes, who would cry out every minute loudly so that all could hear, "I just hope I don't get any mud in my galoshes!" And that is how we arrived at Uncle Hertz's for the Purim dinner.

Although it was still broad daylight, Uncle Hertz's house was brightly illuminated by lamps on the table and by wall sconces. The table was all set. A frighteningly huge Purim bread, as big as the Messianic

Ox, dominated the table, around which stood our family, all the uncles and all the aunts and all the cousins, all, blessed be His name, poor folks, one more so, one less so, all conversing awkwardly in hushed tones amongst themselves, waiting, as at a *bris* waiting for the godfather to carry in the baby. Uncle Hertz was nowhere to be seen, and his wife, a woman with white pearls, dark lips, and false teeth, was fussing busily at the table, straightening the dishes and counting heads with her left hand.

Then all at once the door opened, and there was my Uncle Hertz himself, dressed in his holiday best—a long, shiny silk coat with very broad sleeves, and a fur-trimmed hat that he wore only at the Purim dinner and at the Pesach seder. The whole family bowed to him, the men smiling queerly, rubbing their hands together. The women wished him a happy holiday, and we youngsters remained standing like oafs, not knowing what to do with our hands. With a fierce, intent gaze from behind his silver spectacles, Uncle Hertz examined us one by one from head to toe. He gave a little cough as he did so and motioned with his hand.

"Why aren't you sitting? Sit down, there are chairs."

The whole family sat down, each at the edge of his seat, afraid to touch the table lest he do some damage. A formidable silence prevailed in the room. One could hear the candles burning. Their glow shimmered in our eyes, and our hearts felt gloomy. Although we were hungry, we had lost our appetites, as if an unseen hand had taken them away.

"Why are you all so quiet? Say something, tell something!" commanded Uncle Hertz, and he gave a little cough accompanied by a shrug of the shoulders, a toss upward of the head, and a pursing of the lips.

The family remained silent. No one dared utter a word at Uncle Hertz's table. The men had awkward, foolish grins on their faces, wanting to say something but not knowing what; the women exchanged wild-eyed, wordless glances; and we children burned as if with fever. My sisters looked at one another as if they didn't know each other. My brother, Moshe-Abraham, looked at everything with a pale, terrified face. Not one, not one, dared utter a word at Uncle Hertz's table. But someone did feel at ease here, as he did everywhere and always. That was my Miriam-Reyzl's fiancé, the clerk. He drew the large, starched, smelly handkerchief from his back pocket, blew his nose loudly as if he were at home, and blurted out, "So much mud at Purim! I thought I would get my galoshes full. . . ."

"Who is that young man, ha?" Uncle Hertz asked, raising his silver spectacles with a little cough, a shrug of the shoulders, a toss of the head upward, and a pursing of the lips.

"It's my—my fiancé—my Miriam-Reyzl's fiancé . . ." my father attempted in a weak voice like that of a person confessing he had murdered someone, and we all remained sitting as if stricken, and Miriam-Reyzl—oh, my! Miriam-Reyzl was aflame like a straw roof!

Uncle Hertz studied the whole family with his fierce gray eyes, granted us another little cough, a shrug of the shoulders, a toss of the head upward, and a pursing of the lips, and said to us, "So? Why don't you all go wash up? Go wash your hands, there's water."

After washing, and saying the prayer for the washing of the hands, the family sat down again, and we waited for Uncle Hertz to make the blessing over the bread, the *hamotzi,* and to cut into the huge Purim loaf. In the meantime we sat wordlessly, like mutes, wanting desperately to put something in our mouths. But Uncle Hertz, wouldn't you know, went on at great length, like an overly pious Jew, like a veritable rabbi. At long last, the Purim loaf was slaughtered, but before we could swallow the first bite, Uncle Hertz was already glaring at the whole family with his fierce gray eyes, giving his little cough, his shrug of the shoulders, his toss of the head upward, his pursing of the lips, and saying, "So? Why don't you sing something? Sing a tune in honor of the dinner—after all, it's Purim all over the world!"

The whole family looked from one to the other in a panic and started to whisper something to one another quietly, negotiating over who should start singing. "Sing something." "You sing." "Why me?"

"Why not you?" Finally a tune emerged from one of our family, Abram'l, Uncle Itzi's son, a beardless young man who kept blinking his eyes. Although he had a weak, squeaky voice, he thought he could sing.

What kind of tune Abram'l had in mind to sing, I will never know. I only know that he clutched his Adam's apple, and out came a squeaky sound in a gurgly, high-pitched voice, while he made such a ridiculous, pitiable face that one had to be a god or an angel to be able to hold oneself in without exploding in laughter. And into the bargain, right across from me sat the other children, making such faces that you had to be stronger than iron not to burst out laughing.

The first outburst came from me, and the first slap came from my mother. But the slap did not cool me off. On the contrary, it provoked in all of us youngsters, myself included, a fresh wave of laughter, and the fresh wave of laughter provoked another slap, and after that slap another outburst of laughter, until they dragged me out of the room into the kitchen, from the kitchen outside, and from there brought me home, half dead, beaten up, disheveled, drenched with the bitter tears that were pouring down my face. That evening I cursed myself, cursed Purim, cursed the dinner, cursed Abram'l, and more than anyone, Uncle Hertz, may he forgive me. He is long since gone.

On his grave in our cemetery stands a tombstone,

and on the tombstone engraved in gold letters are all the fine qualities he possessed during his lifetime:

"Here lies—*po nikvar*—an honest man, a philanthropist; good, charitable, loving, generous, considerate, devoted, trustworthy, a great benefactor, friendly," and more and more. "May he rest in peace."

◆ THREE ◆

Chanukah Money

• One •

Guess, children, which holiday is the best holiday of all?

Chanukah, of course!

Eight days in a row with no school, eating *latkes* with goose fat, playing at *dreydl*, and receiving Chanukah money from everyone—so, I ask you, could there be a better holiday?

Winter. Outdoors it is cold; the frost burns fiercely, the windows are frozen over, decorated with beautiful frost trees, and inside, the house is cozy and warm. The silver Chanukah menorah has stood ready since early morning. Father paces from room to room, his hands clasped behind him as he recites the evening prayers. After standing still for the Eighteen Benedictions, he removes from a table drawer a wax candle, the *shamesh,* to light the others with, and as he recites the concluding prayer, he signals to me and my younger brother, Mottel, for he is forbidden to speak until the prayer is over.

"Ee-aw! *Shehu noteh shamayim vayosed haaretz*—He stretched forth the heavens and laid the foundations of the earth—Ee-nu-aw!"

Mottel and I do not understand what he means, and we ask:

"What do you want? A match?"

Father points toward the kitchen.

"Ee-aw-aw! *V'al keyn n'kaveh l'kho*—We therefore hope in Thee—Ee-aw-nu!"

"What? A bread knife? A pair of scissors?"

"Mm-ay-ee-aw-nu-feh! *Bayom hahu yihyeh adonoy ekhud u'shmo ekhod*—On that day the Lord shall be One, and His name One. . . . Your mother! Call your mother, let her hear the blessing over the Chanukah candles."

My brother and I tear out of the room, almost falling over each other.

"Mama! Hurry, Chanukah candles!"

"Oy, God help me, Chanukah candles!" exclaims my mother, abandoning all her work in the kitchen (dressing geese, rendering goose fat, frying *latkes*), and hurries out into the parlor. And right behind her is Brayne, the scullery maid, a swarthy woman with a mustache, a full face, and forever-greasy hands.

Mother stands off to the side and takes on a pious expression while Brayne, the scullery maid, remains standing at the door, wiping her greasy hands on her soiled apron and smearing her nose with her greasy hand, thus leaving a black smudge across her whole face. We have to be stronger than iron, I and my brother, Mottel, to hold ourselves in and not burst out laughing.

Father holds the lit *shamesh* candle near the Chanukah menorah, leans over, and chants the blessing in the familiar tune: "*Boruch atoh!*—Blessed art Thou!," and finishes with, "*l'hadlik nair shel chanukah!*—to kindle the Chanukah candles."

Mother responds with awe in her voice, "*Borukh hu u'borukh sh'mo, amen,*—Blessed be He and blessed be His name, amen," and Brayne nods her head in approval, all the while making such odd faces that I and my brother, Mottel, are afraid to look at each other.

"*Haneyros haleylo sh'onu madlikin*—the candles that we kindle tonight," Father sings under his breath as he paces back and forth around the room, glancing at the Chanukah menorah and praying and praying on and on at great length. We are hoping for it to end soon so he will put his hand in his pocket and take out his purse. We exchange winks and nudge one another.

"Mottel, you go over and ask him for Chanukah money."

"How come *I* have to ask for Chanukah money?"

"Because you're younger, so *you* have to ask for Chanukah money."

"Maybe it's the other way around. You're older, so *you* have to ask for Chanukah money."

Father knows all too well that we are whispering about Chanukah money, but he pretends not to hear. Calmly, unhurriedly, he goes over to the table drawer and begins counting money. A little shiver passes over our bodies, our hands tremble, our hearts pound. We look up at the ceiling, scratch behind our sidelocks, and try to look indifferent, as if this has nothing to do with us.

Father gives a little cough. "Hm . . . children, come over here."

"What? What's the matter?"

"Here's your Chanukah money."

Now that we have our Chanukah money, off we run, I and my brother, Mottel, at first slowly, composed and well mannered, but then faster and faster, with a hop and a skip and a jump. By the time we reach our room we can barely control ourselves. We do three handsprings each and hop on one foot as we chant:

> *Eynge, beynge,*
> *Stupe tzeynge,*
> *Artze, bartze,*
> *Gole shvartze,*
> *Eymeli, reymeli,*

Beygeli, feygeli—
Hup!

Out of great joy and elation, we slap ourselves
twice on the cheeks.

The door opens and in comes Uncle Benny.

"Hey, you scamps, I owe you Chanukah money!"

Uncle Benny puts his hand in his vest pocket,
takes out two silver gulden, and gives us our Chanukah money.

• Two •

No one on earth would ever think that Father and
Uncle Benny were brothers. Father is tall and thin,
while Uncle Benny is short and chubby; Father is
dark, Uncle Benny fair; Father is somber and untalk-
ative, Uncle Benny jolly and a chatterer. They are
as different as night and day, summer and winter, yet
they are brothers.

Father gets a large sheet of paper, rules off black
and white squares, and asks for black and white beans
from the kitchen. This will serve as a checker game.

Mother is in the kitchen rendering goose fat and
frying *latkes*. I and my brother, Mottel, are playing at
dreydl, spinning the dreydl to see which word—Nes
Godol Haya Shom—will appear when it stops spinning, and Father and Uncle Benny sit down to play
checkers.

"There's just one thing I must insist on, Benny: No

changing your mind, do you hear! Once you make a move, it's final!" says Father.

"A move is a move," says Uncle Benny, and makes a move.

"A move is a move," agrees Father, and takes one of Benny's checkers.

"A move is a move," says Uncle Benny, and takes two of Father's checkers.

The longer the game goes on, the more deeply engrossed in the game they become, chewing on their beards, jiggling their legs under the table, and both humming the same tune as they consider their next moves.

"Oy, what to do, what to do, what to do?" chants Father with a tune from the Gemorah while gnawing at the tip of his beard. "If I move here, he'll move there. If I move there, he'll move here. So I had better make this move!"

"What a move, what a move!" Uncle Benny helps him out in the same tune.

"Why should I be afraid?" Father sings on. "If he takes my checker, I'll take two of his. Aha! But what if he has in mind to take three of my checkers?"

"Three checkers, three checkers, three checkers?" Uncle Benny joins in.

"Oy, you're a fool, Benny, a fool and a great one!" sings Father, and makes a move.

"You're a fool yourself, brother, and an even greater one!" sings Uncle Benny, making a move and immediately grabbing his checker back.

"Feh, Benny, I thought we decided, a move is a move!" says Father, now without a tune, and grabs Uncle Benny's hand.

"That didn't count!" protests Uncle Benny. "So long as I'm still making a move, I can go wherever I please!"

"No!" exclaims Father. "A move is final! We did decide that, Benny. No changing your mind, Benny!"

"No changing your mind?" says Uncle Benny. "How many times do you change your mind?"

"I?" says Father. "Eh, Benny, that's why I hate to play checkers with you!"

"So who is forcing you to play with me?"

"Already? You're fighting over a little bean again?" Mother cries, and comes in from the kitchen, her face aflame, and in her footsteps, Brayne, bearing a large platter of steaming *latkes* drenched in goose fat. We all head for the table. I and my brother, Mottel, who just before had been scrapping like cat and dog, quickly make peace and sit down to eat the *latkes* with great gusto.

• Three •

At night I lie on my bed and think: How much would it add up to if, let us say, all the uncles and all the aunts and all the other relatives were to give me Chanukah money? First of all there is Uncle Moshe-Aaron, Mother's brother, tightfisted but a rich man. Then there's Uncle Itzi and Aunt Dvoyra, with whom Father and Mother have been angry for years and years. And what about Uncle Beynish and Aunt Yente? And let's not forget our sister, Eydel. And her husband, Sholem-Zeydel. And all the other relations.

"Mottel, are you sleeping?"

"Yes. What is it?"

"How much do you think Uncle Moshe-Aaron will give us for Chanukah money?"

"How would I know? Am I a prophet?"

A minute later: "Mottel, are you sleeping?"

"Yes. What is it?"

"Does anyone else in the world have as many uncles and aunts as we do?"

"Maybe yes, maybe no."

Two minutes later: "Mottel, are you sleeping?"

"Yes. What is it?"

"If you're sleeping, how can you talk to me?"

"You're asking me questions, so I have to answer you."

Three minutes later: "Mottel, are you sleeping?"

"Tsss-trrr-khilkhilkhil-tsss . . ."

Mottel is snoring, gurgling, whistling through his nose, and I sit up in my bed, take out my money, smooth it out, and examine it.

Just think, I say to myself, It's only a piece of paper, yet what can't you buy with it: toys, penknives, little canes, purses, nuts and sweets, raisins and carob—whatever you want.

I hide my money under my pillow and say my night

prayers, and Brayne comes in from the kitchen bearing a full platter of money. Brayne is not walking, but floating on air, chanting, *"hanayros halaylo sh'onu madlikin. . . ."* and Mottel is swallowing rubles as if they were stuffed cabbages. "Mottel!" I yell with all my might, "God help you, Mottel, what are you doing? *Rubles?"*

I wake up and spit three times to ward off evil. "Tfoo-tfoo-tfoo—a dream!"

And I fall back asleep.

• *Four* •

The following morning after prayers and breakfast, Mother dresses us in our little fur-lined jackets and bundles us up in large, warm shawls, and we are on our way to collect Chanukah money, first, as always, from Uncle Moshe-Aaron.

Uncle Moshe-Aaron is not a well man. He is always suffering from indigestion; whenever you come, you always find him at the washstand, wiping his hands and muttering a prayer, *asher yotzer.*

"Good morning, Uncle Moshe-Aaron!" we both cry out together, I and my brother, Mottel, as we are met by Aunt Pessl, a tiny woman with one eye black and the other white. I should say, one eyebrow black, the other white. Aunt Pessl removes our jackets and unwinds us from our shawls and blows our noses in her apron.

"Blow!" says Aunt Pessl. "Good, good, blow!

Don't hold back! More! More! That's the way!"

Uncle Moshe-Aaron, wearing a quilted yarmulke on his head and an old fur frock coat, with cotton stuffed in his ears and with a sparse mustache, is at the washstand drying his hands, grimacing, blinking his eyes, and straining as he says his prayers.

I and my brother, Mottel, sit down in agony. We always have feelings of dread and chills whenever we come here. Aunt Pessl sits down opposite us, clasps her hands over her heart, and starts to grill us.

"How is your father?"

"Fine."

"How is your mother?"

"Fine."

"Did she dress the geese?"

"Dressed."

"Rendered goose fat?"

"Rendered."

"Fried *latkes*?"

"Fried."

"Uncle Benny visited?"

"Visited."

"Played checkers?"

"Played."

And so on.

Aunt Pessl blows our noses again and says to Uncle Moshe-Aaron, "Moshe-Aaron, you need to give them some Chanukah money."

Uncle Moshe-Aaron doesn't hear; he is still drying his hands, straining to finish his prayers.

Aunt Pessl isn't loath to remind him again. "Moshe-Aaron, Chanukah money for the children!"

"Hah? What?" Uncle Moshe-Aaron sputters, moving the cotton from one ear to the other.

"Chanukah money for the children!" Aunt Pessl shouts right into his ear.

"Oy, my sto-omach! My sto-omach!" Uncle Moshe-Aaron draws the word out painfully and grabs his stomach with both hands. "It's Chanukah money you want? Why do children need money? What will you do with money? Hah? Squander it, throw it away, hah? How much Chanukah money did your father give you? Hah?"

"A ruble for me," I say, "and half a ruble for him."

"A ruble? Hm . . . they spoil kids rotten, they ruin them! What will you do with the ruble? Hah? Spend it? Hah? Don't spend it! Do you hear what I'm telling you? Don't spend it! Maybe you want to spend it, hah?"

"Spend it or not spend it, what difference does it make to you?" Aunt Pessl breaks in. "Give them what they're supposed to get, and let them go in peace."

Uncle Moshe-Aaron goes off to his room, shuffling In his slippers, searches through all the drawers and cupboards, and scrapes out a few small coins, muttering to himself:

"Hm . . . they spoil children rotten, they ruin them, utterly ruin them!"

He shoves a few old coins into our palms. Aunt

Pessl puts on our jackets, wraps us in the large, warm shawls, and we are on our way.

We dash across the white, frozen, crackly snow and try to count the old coins that Uncle Moshe-Aaron has shoved into our hands, but we cannot manage it. Our hands are frozen, red, stiff. The coins are large, heavy, copper coins, the six-ers from olden times, the three-ers worn thin, the groschens old-fashioned, thick, and moldy. It is difficult, impossible, to figure up in the frost how much Chanukah money Uncle Moshe-Aaron has given us!

• Five •

Our second stop for collecting Chanukah money is at Uncle Itzi and Aunt Dvoyra, the ones Mother and Father have been angry with for years and years. Why they are angry, we do not know. We only know that Father and Uncle Itzi (blood brothers) never speak to one another, even though they both pray at the same synagogue and both sit right next to each other on the same bench, cheek by jowl. When a holiday comes and the Torahs are taken from the Ark and the auctioning begins for selling the *aliyas*, the special honors for blessing the Torah, they always try to out-bid each other, both wanting to recite the very same blessing. At that time the synagogue is filled with the excitement of a carnival, everyone talking, nudging one another, whispering, laughing, and egging on the bidders. Everyone is eager to find out which one will win *shishi*, the sixth blessing before the reading of the Torah, or the *moftir*, the reading of the lesson from the Prophets. When the bidding begins to heat up, the congregation urges them to bid to the limit. The *shamesh*, the sexton, Mekhtshi Funfatch, with the red elflocks, stands on the dais bent over, his prayer shawl constantly slipping down his shoulders, his yarmulke awry; he glances toward the eastern wall, where Father and Uncle Itzi are seated, and he chants in his nasal voice, "Eighteen gulden for the sixth honor! Twenty gulden for the sixth honor! Twenty-two gulden for the sixth honor!"

Father and Uncle Itzi sit, one facing this way, one facing that, both pretending to be absorbed in their texts, but whatever one bids, the other tops. The congregation is enjoying every minute of this rivalry and joins in gleefully, "Thirty, thirty! Thirty-five! Thirty-seven! Forty, forty!"

Mekhtshi Funfatch looks from one to the other. "Forty gulden for the sixth honor! Forty-two gulden for the sixth honor! Forty-five gulden for the sixth honor!"

Father and Uncle Itzi continue to outbid each other. They are already up to fifty gulden. Mekhtshi raises his hand and is about to conclude the bidding in favor of Father, "Fifty guld—en!"

But Uncle Itzi reconsiders and raises a finger, the congregation all helping out: "Fifty-one! Fifty-one!" And on it goes, until at long last, the bidding has reached some sixty gulden (no one has ever heard of such an amount!) and the sixth honor belongs to Uncle Itzi. When it is time to auction off the *moftir*, Father looks at the *shamesh* and signals with his hand to indicate that the *moftir* is *his*! For Mekhtshi this is fine, but you can be sure the congregation isn't in agreement. You have to bid, that's the way it is. That's why it's a holiday. There's no monopoly, no automatic claim on the *moftir*!

"Ten gulden for the *moftir*! Fifteen gulden for the *moftir*! Twenty gulden for the *moftir*! Fifty gulden for the *moftir*!"

Quite a jump! Father turns his head. Who is this intruding into his *moftir*? You can guess it is again Uncle Itzi vying with Father; he wants to buy the *moftir* for his young son-in-law. Oh no you don't! You can't have both the *shishi* and the *moftir*! Two honors is one too many! Father stands, and winks to the *shamesh*.

"A hundred!"

The word *hundred* flies through the synagogue like thunder and lightning. The entire congregation is stunned, amazed. Such a high bid for a *moftir* has not been offered since the synagogue has been in existence.

And Mekhtshi forges on with his job. "A hundred gulden for *moftir*! A hundred gulden for *moftir*! A hundred guld—en . . ." (He is eager to close the bidding.)

Uncle Itzi stands up. Father gives him a strange look, as if saying, Are you crazy or out of your mind? Is it a fight you want? Then let's fight!

Uncle Itzi sits down, and the *moftir* remains ours. . . .

Still and all, when there is a family celebration at our house or at Uncle Itzi's—a birth, a bar mitzvah, a *bris*, a *pidyn haben*, an engagement party, a calling to the Torah on the day of a wedding, a marriage or a divorce—they each go to one anothers' homes; each has a seat of honor, they exchange gifts, wish one another well, and dance together with all the family in a circle.

"A good morning to you, Uncle Itzi! A good morning to you, Aunt Dvoyra!" we exclaim together, I and my brother, Mottel, and we are taken up as very welcome guests.

"I'm sure you two aren't here to recite the Haggadah, but for something else. . . ." Uncle Itzi says to us. He pinches our cheeks, takes out his little change purse, and gives us Chanukah money, for me a bright silver twenty-kopek piece, and for my brother, Mottel, a bright silver twenty-kopek piece, and we are on our way to Uncle Beynish's house.

• Six •

If you can imagine a true hell, that is Uncle Beynish's house. No matter when you arrive, you will find complete bedlam, utter chaos, earsplitting noise. There is a house full of children: half-naked, filthy, hair-unwashed, bruised, scratched-up, sickly children with dark circles under their eyes. This one is laughing and that one is crying, this one is singing and that one is shrieking, this one is whooping and that one is whistling, this one is wearing his father's coat with its sleeves rolled up and that one is riding on a broomstick, this one is drinking milk from a pitcher and that one is cracking nuts, this one is walking around with a herring head and that one is sucking a candy as two rivulets flow from his nose into his mouth. Aunt Yente has to be stronger than iron to be able to endure this crew. She curses them, she pinches them, she grabs them hard. She isn't picky; whoever is close at hand is the one who receives the slap, the shove, the poke in the side.

A slap is commonplace. "Choke! The devil take you!" are minor curses; it is not unusual to hear words like *plague, cholera,* and *convulsions,* and yet somehow they are spoken with good humor, in the same tone as if she were saying, "Good Shabbos."

The only time it gets quiet is when Uncle Beynish comes home. But as Uncle Beynish is a very busy man, tending his shop all day and coming home only for a quick bite to eat, the house is always in an uproar.

As we arrive, we find Ezriel'ke (the middle one) riding astride Getzi (the eldest), with Froyke and Mendel (two younger ones) whipping them on, one

with the sleeve of a cotton shirt, the other with the cover of some prayer book. Chaym'l (a middle child between Froyke and Mendel) has found the windpipe of a slaughtered goose, has inflated it with his last breath until he is almost blue in the face, and has managed to produce a weird squeal from it like that of a stuck pig. Zeinvil'le (I don't know whether he is an older or younger child) is playing a concert on a comb, and Duvid'l (a little four-year-old), wearing his boots on his hands, is beating time on the floor with them. Sender'l is carrying a kitten by the scruff of the neck, its little tongue sticking out, its eyes shut, its legs outstretched, as if saying: Look what they do to me! They torture me, torture me!

Esther'l (the oldest girl) wants to comb Khaski's (the younger girl's) hair, to make a braid, but as Khaski's hair is very thick and curly and has gone long uncombed, she refuses, and is crying lustily as she receives slap after slap from her sister. The only quiet one is Pinny'le, a tiny lad with bowed legs, with one shirttail out of his trousers. The problem with him is that wherever he stops, he leaves a little bit of evidence that he's been there. But none of this bothers Aunt Yente. She sits calmly at the table with two infants, one nursing, the other sitting on her lap, as she sips her chicory.

"May God bless your little bones!" she croons fondly to the suckling baby, and clasps it lovingly closer to her breast while shoving the elder one on her lap roughly. "Look at the way you're eating, may the worms eat *you*! Esther'l, Rakh'tzi, Khaski, where are you when I need you? Quick, wipe his nose; wash a saucer out for me, I'm drinking without a saucer! Give him a smack for me that he'll really feel! Dear heart of mine, my soul, my joy! Their mouths never shut! All morning long all they do is eat, may the devil take them!"

When they see me and my brother, Mottel, the children fall on us like locusts, some grabbing our hands, some our legs, some our heads. Chaym'l lets the air out of the inflated goose-windpipe right into my ear, and Duvid'l grabs me around the waist with both boots. Tiny Pinny'le with the shirttail out of his trousers latches on to one of my legs, winding himself around it like a snake, and a pandemonium of shouts envelops us in a loud din.

"May your teeth hurt from screaming!" cries Aunt Yente from the other room. "A person can go deaf around here! They're devils, not children, may their souls burn!"

Aunt Yente screams and the children scream—everyone screams. Suddenly Uncle Beynish arrives with his tallis and tefillin—his prayer shawl and phylacteries—apparently coming from the prayer house. In a split second there is absolute silence, and the entire gang vanishes from sight.

"A good morning to you, Uncle Beynish!" we exclaim, I and my brother, Mottel.

"What are you scamps doing here? I'll bet you're after some Chanukah money!" Uncle Beynish says, taking out his purse and handing us a silver ten-kopek coin.

The children peek out from the corners of the room like cockroaches, stare at us like little mice, wink at us and signal with their fingers while making funny faces to get us to laugh. We barely contain ourselves, and flee from this hell.

We continue on our way for Chanukah money to our sister, Eydel.

Our sister, Eydel, and her husband, Sholem-Zeydel, may they rest in peace, are long in the Next World.

Since early childhood, Eydel was always a weepy soul; over the least little nothing she would cry her heart out, shedding copious tears for her own as well as for others' woes. But once she became engaged to Sholem-Zeydel, she never ceased crying. Perhaps you think it was because she wasn't pleased with her bridegroom? God forbid! Did she know him enough not to be pleased with him? It was simply assumed a bride must cry before the wedding. When the tailors brought the wedding dress to be fitted, she wept all night. Later on, at the engagement party given by her girlfriends—when they began the dancing, she kept running off to her room to bury her head in her pillow for a good cry. Don't even *ask* about what happened on the day of the wedding! That was *her* day.

She never stopped crying. But the supreme moment came at the veiling ceremony, when Menasha Fiddele, the *klezmer*, seated her on the bridal chair and Reb Boruch, the *bodkhin*, the traditional entertainer of brides who prepares them for the reality of married life, mounted the table, folded his hands across his stomach, lowered his head as one does when grieving the dead, and sang a beautiful mournful tune that would have moved a stone to tears:

Dear bride! Lovely bride!
Let your tears flow,
Let them stream from your eyes,
Let your sad beauty show.
Soon you will stand beneath the canopy,
Your head bowed low
In innocence before the wedding vows.
But after, you will too soon know
What the rest have known for a long, long time:
Our lives are full of bitterness
Here below.
A human being is not made of stone
But of ache and woe,
Of flesh and blood,
Through and through.
The wicked suffer whippings in hell,
Blow upon blow,
Their weeping and wailing and crying out
Grow and grow.
You must yourself be virtuous,
Hold yourself low.

Let your tears be humble,
Let your sad eyes flow.

And in this mode he went on and on.

All the women, both relatives and friends, who stood hovering over her, helping unloosen the bride's lovely, thick hair, made ridiculous faces, pursed their lips, blew their noses, and wiped their eyes while poor Eydel wailed and sobbed, carrying on so that she fainted three times and was barely revived with great effort.

But as weepy as our sister was, our brother-in-law, Sholem-Zeydel, was cheerful, lively, a practical joker, a wag, and, may he forgive me, a pain in the neck. He loved to tease, to flick other people's noses or ears—he thought that was the greatest fun. How many times did we, I and my brother, Mottel, go around with throbbing ears. We were thrilled to death when we heard that the two of them would no longer be supported by my father in our house and would be moving to their own place. The day they moved, our house was in a state of utter chaos. Eydel was in tears, bemoaning her fate, while Mother joined her. And Sholem-Zeydel, who was going through the motions of packing their belongings, kept leaping about, slyly stealing up on us for a flick to the tip of the nose or to the back of the ear. He finally left, and had the audacity to tell us not to wait long for an invitation but to be frequent visitors! We promised ourselves never to set eyes on him again!

But people forget everything, especially a flick on the nose. How could we not go for Chanukah money to our own brother-in-law?

When we arrive at Eydel's, Sholem-Zeydel greets us with a broad "Look who's here! What's the good word? You did the right thing to come here. I've got some Chanukah money for you!"

And Sholem-Zeydel removes from his change purse some coins and places a few newly minted, shiny silver coins right into our palms, and before we even have a chance to count them out, we have received several flicks, first I to the tip of the nose and then Mottel to the back of the ear, then Mottel to the tip of the nose and I to the back of the ear.

"Stop tormenting these poor children!" our sister, Eydel, pleads with tears in her eyes. She draws us off to the side and fills our pockets with honey cake, nuts, and carob and throws in some extra Chanukah money.

We take to our heels and race home.

• *Seven* •

"So, Mottel, let's get to work and figure out how much Chanukah money we have. But do you know what? You be quiet; first I'll count out my share, and then you count yours."

And I count: "A ruble and three twenty-kopek pieces, and four zlotys, and five grivnis, and six pitakes. How much does that make? Looks like it's a ruble and three twenty-kopek pieces, four zlotys, five grivnis, and six pitakes. . . ."

My brother, Mottel, can't wait till I add mine all up, and he begins adding up *his* haul; he transfers the coins from one hand to the other, counting, "A twenty-kopek piece and a twenty-kopek piece comes to two twenty-kopek pieces, plus another twenty-kopek piece adds up to three twenty-kopek pieces, plus two gulden are three twenty-kopek pieces and two gulden, and a grivni plus another grivni and another grivni—comes to two twenty-kopek pieces, three gulden, I mean three gulden and two twenty-kopek pieces. Tphoo! What am I talking about? I have to start all over again from the beginning!"

And he begins from the beginning. We add and add and it doesn't add up. We count and count and it doesn't come out right. When we get to Uncle Moshe-Aaron's old pitakes, heavy six-kopek coins, rubbed-out three-kopek coins, and fat groschens, we get so mixed up in our counting that we have no way of figuring out what we have. We try to exchange these old coins with Mother, with Father, with Brayne, the cook—it won't work! No one wants to touch them!

"What kind of pitakes are these? Who gave you these old coins?"

We are ashamed to tell who, and remain silent.

"Do you know what I think we should do?" my brother, Mottel, says to me. "Let's take them and throw them into the oven or throw them in the snow so no one will find them."

"Pretty clever!" I say to him. "Wouldn't it be smarter to give them to some beggar?"

But just our luck—no beggar is in sight! What has become of all the beggars who claw at your coattails, who plead with you for another kopek, who curse and harangue? No; once you need something, it will never happen! Never! Never!

◆ FOUR ◆

The Pesach Guest

"**R**eb Yoneh, I have a Pesach guest for you the likes of whom you've never seen in your life!"

"How so?"

"I'll tell you how so. He's a rare bird, not your ordinary Pesach guest!"

"Tell me, what makes him such a rare bird?"

"Give me a chance! By a rare bird I mean he's a pure gem, a magnificent Jew. If he has one fault, it's that he doesn't speak our language."

"What language does he speak?"

"The Holy Tongue."

"Is he from Jerusalem?"

"Where he's from, I don't know, but when he speaks all you hear are long, drawn-out 'aah's."

This conversation took place between my father

and Ezriel, the synagogue caretaker, the *shamesh,* a few days before Passover. I was most eager to lay my eyes on this rare bird who didn't speak our language and talked in long, drawn-out "aah"s. Earlier that day in the synagogue I had spotted this strange being wearing a traditional fur-trimmed cap and a yellow, blue, and red-striped Turkish robe. All of us youngsters drew as close as we could to him in order to give him a good looking-over, for which we earned a scolding from Ezriel, the *shamesh:* "Children shouldn't get into the habit of pestering strangers!"

After the service the entire congregation greeted the newcomer and wished him a happy holiday, and the newcomer responded to each and every one with a sweet smile on his ruddy face, which was bordered with a small gray beard: *"Shaalum! Shaalum!"* His *"Shaalum! Shaalum!"* brought out gales of laughter in us youngsters, so vexing Ezriel, the *shamesh,* that he came at us with his hand raised, ready to strike, but we dodged out of his reach. Again we sneaked around to the newcomer, bursting out laughing, to hear how he said, *"Shaalum! Shaalum!"* and again we had to escape Ezriel's ready hand.

Proud as a peacock I accompanied my father and this personage to our house for the holidays and felt that all my friends were envying me my extraordinary guest. They all followed us with their eyes, and I turned my head and stuck my tongue out at them. All the way home the three of us were silent. Upon entering the house, my father said to my mother, "A good *yontev!*" and the guest nodded his head, the fur hat nodding along. "*Shaalum! Shaalum!*" I immediately thought of my friends and lowered my face toward the table so as not to explode in laughter. I kept peeking at the guest, and I liked what I saw. I liked his yellow, blue, and red-striped Turkish robe; I liked his rosy, blooming cheeks ringed with the neatly trimmed, gray beard; I liked his fine black eyes that peered smilingly from under the thick, gray brows.

I could see that my father also liked him. He was clearly delighting in his guest's company. My mother gazed at him in awe as if he were a holy man. No one spoke. Father himself prepared the guest's seat with its heap of comfortable pillows. Mother was busily preparing the seder meal with the help of Rikl, the maid. At last the time came to say the kiddush blessing, and my father and the guest began conversing in Hebrew. I was fairly bursting with pride because I could understand nearly every word. I will quote exactly, word for word, their Hebrew conversation:

FATHER: *Nu?* (In our language that means: Be so kind as to make the kiddush.)

GUEST: *Nu-nu!* (In our language that means: Please! You do it!)

FATHER: *Nu-o?* (And why not you?)

GUEST: *O-nu?* (And you, why not?)

FATHER: *Ee-o!* (You first!)

GUEST: *O-ee!* (First you!)

FATHER: *Eh-o-ee!* (I beg you, you do it!)

GUEST: *Ee-o-eh!* (You do it, I beg you!)

FATHER: *Ee-eh-o-nu?* (Will it offend you to say it first?)

GUEST: *Ee-o-eh-nu-nu!* (If you insist, I'll do it!)

And the guest took the kiddush cup from my father's hand and chanted a kiddush the likes of which we had not heard before and will never hear again. First, the Hebrew, pronounced with long, drawn-out, "aah"s, and second, the voice. His voice did not emerge from his throat but seemed to emanate from the depths of his yellow, blue, and red-striped Turkish robe. I couldn't help thinking of my friends and what laughter would have erupted and what slaps would have been flying at this kiddush! But as I was here alone, I contained myself, put the Four Questions to my father, and we proceeded to recite the Haggadah all together. I was proud as could be that this personage was our guest and not anyone else's.

The Talmudic scholar who said there should be no talking during mealtimes, may he forgive me, did not know anything about how Jews live. I ask you, when does a Jew have time to speak if not during mealtimes? And especially at the seder, when so much time is devoted to reciting the Haggadah before and after the meal. Once Rikl, the maid, had passed the water pitcher for washing, we made the blessing over the eating of the matzo, *al akhilas matzo,* and my mother served the fish. My father rolled up his sleeves and entered into a long conversation with our guest in Hebrew. The first thing Father asked him was the usual question one Jew asks another, "*Ma sh'maykhem*—what is your name?"

To that the guest replied entirely in long, drawn-out "aah"s and in one breath, as one reels off the ten sons of Haman in the Megillah, "*Aik Bokher Galash Demes Hanakh Vosem Zen Khafef Tatzetz.*"

Father was dumbstruck, his mouth agape as he stared in astonishment at the man who possessed a name of such length. I began coughing and looked down at my feet under the table. My mother warned, "Eat your fish slowly, carefully, or you can choke on a bone, God forbid." She looked at the guest in awe. It seems she was very impressed by the name, even though she could not figure it out. But my father explained it to her.

"You understand, in his country each name begins with the first nine letters of the Hebrew alphabet. For them it is a custom to name everyone according to the letters of the alphabet."

"Alphabet! Alphabet!" echoed the guest with a sweet smile on his rosy cheeks, and his fine black eyes gazed with sincere friendliness at each and every one of us, even at Rikl, the maid.

Once my father had learned his name, he now became curious to find out where he came from. This I figured out by the names of cities and countries I was able to make out and which Father translated for Mother, offering a commentary after almost every one. My mother was greatly impressed by each reference, as was Rikl, the maid. And there was much to be impressed by. It was no small matter: You have to travel about ten thousand miles, crossing seven oceans and a desert, in order to reach his land. It takes no fewer than forty days and forty nights to cross the desert, and when you are almost there, you have to scale a high mountain whose ice-covered peak reaches to the clouds, where terrifying winds howl. A perilous place!

But once safely over this mountain, you see before you a veritable Garden of Eden filled with the aromas of spices and cloves and where they grow all manner of exotic fruit in addition to apples and pears and oranges and grapes and dates and olives and nuts and figs. The houses are built of solid spruce covered with roofs of pure silver, the dishes are of fine gold. (Just then the guest glanced at our silver goblets and the silver spoons, forks, and knives.) Jewels, pearls, and diamonds lie scattered in the streets, and no one takes the trouble to bend down and pick them up because there they have no value. (Just then, the guest glanced at Mother's diamond earrings and the pale yellow pearls at her white throat.)

"Do you hear?" my father said to my mother with delight.

"I hear," my mother answered him, and asked, "Why don't they bring some of it here? They could make a fortune! Go on—ask him, Yoneh."

My father put the question to him and was given

a prompt reply, which he related to my mother in our language. "Understand, he says, when you are there, you can take all you wish, full pockets, but as soon as you leave, you must give everything back, and if they find anything at all on you, you are sentenced to death."

"What do you mean?" my mother asked, horrified.

"That means, they hang you from a tree or stone you to death."

The man's tales grew more and more interesting, and when we had finished eating the soup and dumplings and had begun sipping our wine, Father asked him, "To whom does it all belong? Do you have a king?"

He immediately received a precise answer and conveyed it with great pleasure to my mother in our language.

"He says it all belongs to Jews who are called Sephardim, and they have a king, he says, who is also a Jew, a very pious Jew who wears a large round hat trimmed with fur, he says, and is called Yosef-ben-Yosef. He is the high priest to the Sephardim, and he rides in a golden carriage drawn by six spirited horses, and when he goes to the synagogue, he is greeted with song by Levites.

"Levites sing in your shul?" Father asked him, astonished, and received an immediate response that he gave over to my mother in our language, his face glowing like the sun.

"What do you say to that? He says they have a Holy Temple and priests and Levites and an organ. . . .

"And an altar as well?" Father asked, and was given an answer that he translated for my mother into our language, "He says they have an altar, and sacrifices offered in golden vessels—everything just as it was in the olden days in Jerusalem."

With these words my father let out a deep sigh, and, looking at him, my mother sighed as well. I did not understand what there was to sigh about. On the contrary, we should be proud, we should be happy, that we have a land where a Jewish king, a high priest, reigns and where we can find a Holy Temple with priests, Levites, an organ, an altar, and sacrifices. . . .

Luminous fantasies lifted me upward and transported me far, far away to that place, to that blessed Jewish land where the houses are built of solid spruce, where the roofs are covered with pure silver, where the dishes are made of fine gold, and where jewels, pearls, and diamonds lie scattered on the streets.

An idea crept into my mind: If I were there, I would know what to do. I would know where to hide the riches. They would never find anything on me; I would be able to bring home a fine gift for my mother: diamond earrings and several strands of pearls. I glanced at my mother's diamond earrings and the pale yellow pearls at her white throat, and I felt a powerful longing to be in that land.

I decided that after Pesach I would accompany our guest back to his land, naturally without anyone knowing about it. I would divulge my secret only to the guest. I would pour my heart out to him, tell him the whole truth and beg him to take me with him for only a little while. He would surely do this for me. He was such a good, benevolent person. He gazed in such a friendly way at each and every one of us, even at Rikl, the maid. In such a friendly way!

These were my thoughts as I looked at our guest, and I imagined he knew what I was thinking because he was looking at me with his fine black eyes and I thought he winked at me and was saying to me in his language, Hush, little scamp, just wait till after Pesach and it will all work out!

All night long, dreams spun out in my head: a desert, a Holy Tongue, a high priest, and a tall mountain at whose top jewels, pearls, and diamonds grow on trees, and my friends are shaking the trees, and heaps of jewels, pearls, and diamonds are falling to the ground. And I stand below and stuff my pockets with jewels, pearls, and diamonds; and—miraculously!—no matter how much I cram into my pockets, more and more can go in! I put my hand into my pocket to take some out, but instead of jewels, pearls, and diamonds, I find all kinds of fruits: apples and pears and oranges and olives and dates and nuts and figs.

It somehow fills me with anxiety, and I toss from side to side in my bed, and I dream about the Holy

Temple, and I hear the high priest pronouncing benedictions and the Levites singing and the organ playing, and I have the desire to enter the Holy Temple but cannot—Rikl, the maid, is holding me fast and is not letting me. I beg her, I scream, I weep, I toss from side to side. Finally I awake with a start and . . . Standing before me I saw my father and my mother half-dressed, both pale as death, my father's head bowed, my mother wringing her hands, tears brimming in her lovely eyes. My childish heart sensed that something bad had happened, very bad, but whatever my childish mind could have imagined was nothing compared to what did happen.

Our guest, the personage from the faraway land, from that happy land where the houses are built of solid spruce and covered with pure silver and so on and so forth, had vanished, and with him had vanished much else: all the silver goblets; all the silver spoons, forks, and knives; all of the little jewelry my mother had possessed; as well as money, as much as was to be found in our chest. And Rikl, the maid, had also vanished with him.

My childish heart was breaking, not for the silver goblets and the silver spoons, forks, and knives that had vanished, and not for my mother's jewelry or the money or for Rikl, the maid—to the devil with her!—but for that happy, happy land where jewels, pearls, and diamonds lay scattered in the streets, for the Holy Temple and the high priest and the Levites and the organ and the altar and the sacrifices and all the other glorious things I had been robbed of, that had been taken from me, taken from me, taken from me.

And I turned my face to the wall and wept silently.

FIVE

The Clock

The clock struck thirteen.

Don't think I am joking. I am telling you in all seriousness about something that really happened in Kasrilevka, in our own house, and before my own eyes.

We had a clock, a wall clock, an old, old family heirloom handed down by my grandfather, who inherited it from my great-grandfather, several generations in a row going way back to Chmelnitzki's times. It's a pity, I tell you, that a clock is not a living thing but a mute object that cannot speak. It would have endless stories to tell! In our town our clock had the reputation of being the foremost clock, "Reb Nakhum's clock." Townspeople would come to set their clocks by it because it kept the most accurate time.

You must understand that even Reb Leibish Khakaron, the philosopher, who was an expert on telling time by the setting of the sun and who knew the celestial calendar by heart, was known to have said (I myself heard it from his own mouth) that compared to his own watch, our clock was a piece of trash, not worth a pinch of snuff, but when compared to other clocks, our clock was a *real* clock.

And if Reb Leibish Khakaron himself said that, you could very well believe him, because Reb Leibish Khakaron took great pains every Wednesday evening between *minkha* and *maariv* prayers to climb up the stairs to the roof of the women's shul or to the top of the hill near the old synagogue in order to observe carefully and to capture the exact moment when the sun set. In one hand he would hold his watch; in the other hand, his celestial calendar, and as the sun went down on the other side of Kasrilevka, Reb Leibish would say to himself, "Got it!" Frequently he would come to our house to synchronize the two timepieces. Entering without so much as a "Good evening," he would peer at our wall clock, then at his watch and at the calendar, and again at our wall clock, his watch, and the calendar, several times over—and he would be gone.

But one time when Reb Leibish came to synchronize the timepieces with the calendar, he let out a cry: "Na-khum! Hurry! Where are you?"

My father, more dead than alive with fright, came

dashing in. "What's happened, Reb Leibish?"

"Villain, you're asking *me*?" Reb Leibish stuck his watch right under Father's nose, pointed at our wall clock, and bellowed in the pained voice of a person whose sore finger had just been stepped on, "Na-khum! Why don't you say something? Can't you see it's running a half minute fast, a half min-ute FAST! Throw it OUT!" (The last word was expressed with great emphasis, like the last word of the *sh'ma yisroel's* "and God is ONE!")

My father resented this. Who did Reb Leibish think he was, telling him to throw his clock out?

"How did you come to the conclusion, Reb Lei-bish, that *my* clock is running a half minute *fast*? Could it be just the opposite, that your watch is run-ning a half minute *slow*? Who's to say?"

Reb Leibish looked at my father as at a person who had just said the new moon lasted three days, or that Yom Kippur fell on the night before Pesach, or some-thing so equally unthinkable that if one were to take it seriously, one would surely have a stroke! Reb Lei-bish did not reply. He sighed deeply, spun around without so much as a fare-thee-well, slammed the door behind him, and was gone! But no matter. As the whole town knew, Reb Leibish was the kind of Jew nothing in the world pleased. To him the best cantor was no better than a cabbage, a log. The brightest person was an ox, an ass. The best marriage match was ill-fated, wrong in every way. The cleverest parable held no water. That's the kind of Jew Reb Leibish Khakaron was.

But let me get back to our clock. I tell you, that was *really* a clock! Its chiming could be heard three houses away: *Bomm!* . . . *Bomm!* . . . *Bomm!* . . . Half the town depended on its chiming—at midnight for prayer and study, during the High Holy Days, Friday night to make the blessings on the challa and candles, at the end of the Sabbath to light the fire, to tell us when to salt meat and do the many other rituals important to *Yiddishkayt*. In short, our clock was the town clock. The poor thing served very steadfastly, never losing a second. In its entire existence it had never needed the attention of a clockmaker. Father himself was its only master. He had a special knack for what made a clock tick. Every year, on Passover eve, he would carefully remove it from the wall, clean out its works with a feather duster, and remove from its insides a wad of spiderwebs and dead flies the spiders had lured there and decapitated, as well as nests of dead cockroaches that had wandered in and perished. When it was all cleaned out and shined up, he returned it to the wall, where it shone brightly. In fact, they both shone brightly—the clock, because it had been cleaned and polished, and Father, because the clock shone.

But then one day it happened. It was on a lovely, clear day, and we were all sitting around the table eating lunch. Whenever the clock struck the hour, loved to count along out loud: "One . . . two . . . three . . . seven . . . eleven . . . twelve . . . thirteen . . . What! Thirteen!"

"Thirteen?" Father exclaimed, and burst out laughing. "You're some mathematician, *kayn eyn horeh!* Have you ever heard of a clock striking thirteen?"

"Thirteen," I insisted. "As I am a Jew, it was thirteen!"

"You'll get thirteen slaps from me!" Father replied angrily. "Don't ever say such foolish things again. Dumbbell, a clock *can't* strike thirteen!"

"I hate to say this, Nakhum," Mother contributed, "but I'm afraid the child is right. It seems to me I also counted thirteen!"

"That's great! We have another mathematician!" said Father, himself beginning to have some doubts. After the meal he went over to the clock, stood on a stool, and fiddled around with a little wheel inside, and the clock began to strike. The three of us counted together, nodding along with each chime: "One . . . two . . . three . . . seven . . . nine . . . twelve . . . thirteen . . ."

"Thirteen?" said Father incredulously, and he looked at us with the expression of someone who had suddenly heard the wall begin to speak. Again he fiddled with the same wheel, and again the clock struck thirteen! Father climbed down from the stool with a sigh, pale as death, and remained standing in the middle of the room, gazing at the ceiling, nibbling his beard and muttering to himself, "Struck thirteen. . . . What does that mean? . . . What could be wrong? . . . If it were broken, it would stop. . . . So what then? I have to figure it out. . . . Can it be a spring? . . ."

"Why speculate?" said Mother. "Just take the clock down and fix it. You're the expert!"

"Maybe you have a point there," Father answered. So he removed the clock and began fussing with it. Perspiring, he toiled away at the clock a whole day and hung it back in its place. Thank God, the clock was working again as it was supposed to. At midnight, we all stood in front of the clock, and we all counted off just twelve. Father was delighted.

"Aha! It's not striking thirteen anymore! When I say it's a little spring, I know what I'm talking about!"

"I've always said you had a knack with clocks," Mother remarked. "There's just one thing I can't understand. Why is it rasping? It seems it never rasped that way before."

"You're imagining it!" said Father, but as he listened carefully, the clock rasped just before it began striking. Like an old man just before he coughs, it went, *Khil-khil-khil-trrrr* . . . and then it went *Bomm!* . . . *Bomm!* . . . *Bomm!* But the *bomm* itself was not the same *bomm* as before. The *bomm* that used to be was a cheerful *bomm*, a lively *bomm*. Now there had stolen into it a kind of sadness, a cheerlessness, like the voice of an old, out-of-practice cantor pressed into service on Yom Kippur at the final *ne'ileh* prayer.

The rasping grew louder and the chiming quieter and sadder and Father grew more and more downcast; you could see that it hurt him deeply and he was suffering in silence. It disturbed his well-being, but there was nothing he could do. It seemed the clock would at any moment come to a complete standstill. The pendulum began moving irregularly, haltingly. It swung to one side and seemed to get caught in something, as though it were an old man dragging a lame leg. It was plain that the clock was on its downhill course toward stopping forever, for good! But luckily Father realized it was not the clock's fault. It was the weights—not enough weights! He attached an additional two-pound pestle, and the clock took off like a demon. Father was elated, a new man!

But it didn't last long. Again the clock turned lazy and the pendulum began its strange motions, a slow swing to one side followed by a fast one to the other with a scratchy-sounding *kkhi.* It was heartbreaking, soul-rending to see the clock fading. And poor Father, as he looked at the clock, himself seemed to languish, to fade with grief.

Like a devoted, expert doctor who sacrifices himself for his patient's sake, doing everything in his power, going out of his way to try every possible remedy in order to save the life of his patient, so Father began trying to save the life of the old clock by any and all means.

"Not enough weights, not enough strength!" said Father as he added objects to increase the weight: first an iron frying pan, then a copper pitcher; later an iron, a sack of sand, and two bricks. The clock drew new strength each time. Although in a belabored way and with great difficulty, it did run. But then one night, disaster!

It was winter, Friday night. We had finished eating our Shabbos dinner—the delicious peppered fish with horseradish, the hot chicken soup with noodles, and the prune *tzimmes*—and had said grace as is fitting. The Shabbos candles were still flickering and the maid was serving fresh, warm, delicious, well-dried sunflower seeds from the oven when in came Aunt Yente, a dark-haired, lively woman without teeth whose husband had left her and gone off to America several years back.

"Good Shabbos!" said Aunt Yente. "I knew you would have fresh sunflower seeds. The only problem is, I can't crack the shells. May that scoundrel of a husband of mine have as many years to live as I have teeth in my mouth. How do you like the price of fish nowadays, Malka? What are those fishmongers up to? I ask Menasha, the fishmonger, 'Why are your fish so expensive?' That rich Sora-Pearl jumps in: 'Serve me first, serve me, weigh that pike for me!' 'What's the big hurry,' I say. 'God be with you, it won't run away, and Menasha isn't about to throw the fish back in. For the rich,' I say, 'money is plentiful, but common sense is scarce.' Well, she really opens up a mouth to

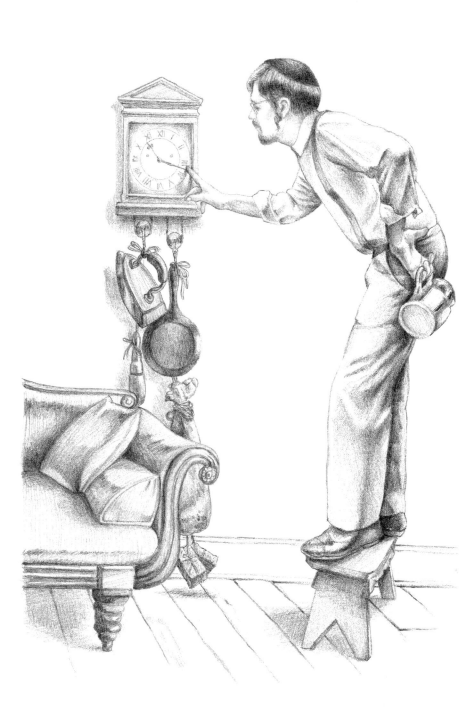

me. 'Poor people,' she says, 'have no business coming here. A poor person,' she says, 'shouldn't go around wanting things she can't afford. . . .' What do you say to that vixen? Not too long ago she was an old maid toiling away in her mother's shop selling ribbons. Just like it happened to Pessil, Peysi-Avrom's daughter. They gloat over their daughter's marriage to a rich man from Strishtch who took her without a groschen to her name. That's Jewish *mazel* for you. They say she's miserable, curses her life, can't get along with the children. Do you think it's easy to be a stepmother? May it not happen to anyone! Now take Khava'le—what do those children have against her? You should see what trouble she has from her stepchildren! Night and day all you hear are insults, curses, smacks a dime a dozen."

The candles began to go out. The shadows on the wall lengthened and climbed higher as the sound of sunflower seeds cracking punctuated the conversation and story-telling, one story casually leading to another. But Aunt Yente was talking more than anyone else.

"Wait!" Aunt Yente cried. "Wasn't there recently an even more interesting story? Not far from Yampele, about three miles, robbers broke into a Jewish inn and murdered everyone in it, including an infant in a cradle. Only one servant girl, who was sleeping in the kitchen on the stove, survived. She heard the screams, sprang off the stove, peeked through a crack in the door, and saw her master and mistress lying dead on the ground in a pool of blood. The girl decided to jump out the nearest window and ran quickly into town screaming at the top of her lungs: "Help, save us, murderers, help!"

Suddenly, as Aunt Yente was carrying on, we heard, *Trrrakh-tarrarrakh-bomm-dzin-dzin-bomm!* . . . Absorbed in her story, we thought robbers had broken into our house and were shooting at us with ten guns, or that the roof had caved in, or that there was an earthquake or some other disaster. We were riveted to our seats. We stared at one another speechless for a moment, and then all of us, as one, began to shout: "Help! Help! Help!"

In a panic, my mother clutched me to her bosom, crying: "My child, let them harm me, not you, God in heaven!"

"Oh! What is it? What's happened? What's the matter with him?" Father exclaimed.

"Nothing, nothing! *Sha! Sha!*" exclaimed Aunt Yente, waving her hands as the servant girl ran in from the kitchen terrified.

"Who's screaming? What's the matter? Is there a fire? Where's the fire? Where?"

"What fire? What are you talking about, silly goose?" Aunt Yente berated the servant girl. "Go back to the kitchen! Why are you all screaming? We had a little fright, that's all! Just a little bang, just the clock—the clock fell down, that's all it was.

You hung too many weights on it, so it fell down. Why such a big fuss? Forgive the comparison, but even if it had been a person, it couldn't do any better. Who ever heard of a clock with so many weights!"

That brought us to our senses. One by one we got up from the table and went over to the poor clock and gazed at how it lay face down, dead, broken, shattered, smashed, mutilated forever beyond repair!

"No more clock!" said Father in a stunned voice, his head lowered as if he were looking at a corpse or saying a prayer for the dead. He wrung his hands, and tears filled his eyes. I looked at my father and felt like crying.

"Come now, why do we need to eat our hearts out?" Mother said gently. "Maybe it was a sign from Above, that today, this very minute, was meant to be the clock's last, like that of a person, forgive the comparison, may God not punish me for these words! I shouldn't say this on the Sabbath, but may it be a redemption for me, for you, for our children, for all our beloved and dear ones, and for all of Israel. Amen *selah*. . . ."

• • •

All night long, clocks filled my dreams. I dreamed that our old clock lay on the ground clad in white shrouds. I dreamed that the clock was alive, and a long tongue, a human tongue, was swaying back and forth in place of the pendulum. The clock was not chiming but groaning, and every groan rent my heart. And on its dial, where I always saw the twelve, I suddenly saw the number thirteen. Really, thirteen—you can truly believe me!

Glossary

BAR MITZVAH: Confirmation ceremony of a male reaching his thirteenth birthday, when a boy comes of age and assumes religious responsibility.

BRIS: Circumcision ceremony of eight-day-old baby boys according to the covenant between God and Abraham.

CHANUKAH: Also called the Festival of Lights, the eight-day-long holiday commemorating the purification of the Temple in Jerusalem by the Maccabees in 167 B.C., marking the successful end to the struggle for religious freedom; celebrated from the twenty-fifth day of Kislev with the lighting of candles, the giving of gifts, the eating of potato pancakes, and the playing of games of chance with the dreydl.

COMMENTARIES: Interpretations of sacred texts.

DREYDL: A four-sided spinning top with a Hebrew letter on each side. The children spin the dreydl and win or lose depending upon which letter is on top when the dreydl stops spinning.

HAGGADAH: Book for the Passover home service during the two consecutive seders on the first two nights of Passover.

KASRILIKES: Poor folks from the fictional town of Kasrilevka.

KAYN EYN HOREH: Literally, no evil eye; the equivalent of knocking on wood when one fears being punished for excessive praise or when one hopes there is truth in one's words.

KIDDUSH: The benediction over the wine at the beginning of the Sabbath or holiday evening meal. Once the person making the prayer has begun, he may not speak until he has completed it and eaten bread.

KLEZMER: Musician.

LATKES: Potato pancakes traditionally eaten during Chanukah.

MATZO: The unleavened flat bread eaten during Passover to commemorate the years the Jews spent wandering through the desert.

MEGILLAH: The Book of Esther, the story of Purim, written on a scroll and read aloud in synagogues on Purim. When the name of the villain, Haman, is spoken, the children drown it out with noisemakers.

MENORAH: Candelabrum holding the nine candles for Chanukah.

MESSIANIC OX: Known as the *shor-habor*. According to

Jewish lore, the legendary gigantic ox that will provide endless food for the righteous when the Messiah comes.

MINKHA-MAARIV: The daily afternoon and evening prayers.

PESACH: Passover, the spring festival celebrated for eight days, commemorating the Jews' exodus from Egypt, where they were slaves.

PIDYEN HABEN: Redemption of the first-born male. The child is symbolically redeemed from the Priest (a Kohen), to whom, according to ancient Jewish law, the child rightfully "belongs." There is usually a small celebration to mark this event.

PURIM: An early spring festival, celebrating the downfall of Haman, the villain who tried to destroy the Jews, as told in the Book of Esther. It is a joyous holiday, marked by feasts, parades, and costume parties, exchanges of baked goods and sweets, and dramatic renditions of the Purim story.

REB: Mister.

SEDER: The festive meal eaten on the first two nights of Passover. The Haggadah is read around the family seder table. The Four Questions are asked by the youngest child and answered by all present; the Passover story is told; four glasses of wine are drunk; matzos, chopped apples, parsley, and eggs are eaten to symbolize the various aspects of the history of the Jews fleeing Egypt and their subsequent liberation.

SEPHARDIM: Jews of medieval Spain or Portugal or descendants of those Jews.

SHABBOS: Sabbath, starting at sundown Friday night

and ending at sundown Saturday night. The day of rest and worship for Jews.

SHALOM: Literally, *peace*. Used as a Jewish word of greeting or farewell.

SHAMESH: Sexton or caretaker in a synagogue, rabbi's personal assistant; also the candle used to light the other candles of the menorah during Chanukah.

SH'MA YISROEL: "Hear O Israel," the credo of Jews, the prayer recited daily.

"SHOSHANAS YAAKOV": Popular Purim song.

SHUL: Synagogue, school, prayer room.

TALLIS: Prayer shawl.

TALMUD: A compilation of the religious, ethical, and legal teachings and decisions of the rabbis interpreting the Bible.

TEFILLIN: Phylacteries; square leather boxes containing scriptural passages worn on the left arm and forehead during weekday morning prayers by observant male Jews over thirteen.

TZIMMES: Carrots, simmered in honey or sugar, with prunes and potatoes.

YARMULKE: Small head-covering worn at all times by observant Jewish males.

YIDDISHKAYT: Jewishness, the essence of being Jewish.

YOM KIPPUR: Day of Atonement; the most important Jewish holiday, a day of fasting and solemn prayer. Takes place eight days after Rosh Hashanah, together called High Holy Days.

YONTEV: Contraction for *yom tov*, or holiday.